WHEN YOUR SOUL TO GLIDE

THE POETRY OF RUSSELL C. BRENNAN

December Books

LIMITED EDITION BOOK

Published by December Books UK

Copyright © 2022 Russell C. Brennan All Rights Reserved.

Cover photo and design by Russell C. Brennan

(Front cover model Maiko)

No part of this book may be reproduced in any form or by any electronic or mechanical means including information storage and retrieval systems, without permission in writing from the author. The only exception is by a reviewer, who may quote short excerpts in a review.

Author website: http://dedicated-follower.co.uk/rcb.html

Website: http://dedicated-follower.co.uk/December-Books.html

Email: december.books@yahoo.com

All photos in the book are by Russell

except The Honeycombs one

All reasonable efforts were taken to find copyright owners of this photo

If you own it please get in touch to be credited.

All others © Russell C. Brennan

INTRODUCTION

A POETRY BOOK BY GEISHA & MULTI-PLATFORM ARTIST RUSSELL C. BRENNAN

Welcome to what is effectively my 3rd book of poems. This one is different to the other two, in that it concerntrates on the words, the other two were photos/art with lyrics /poems sharing equal space, because I am also an established photographer & artist. Having said that, I have put a few small photos in as I felt it did need something a bit extra but they are not the focus of proceedings like the previous book.
You may be wondering by now why I am listed as a Geisha? The word means total artist or multi-platform artist and I have made a dent in all the arts as well as being influenced by Japan and like many Geishas am considered a walking work of art.

Why break from my winning formula of limited edition books featuring poems & photos? Like the only other male Geisha, sadly no longer with us since he left this black star, I am always evolving and often do the unexpected, so thought I would see if a poetry only book would be welcomed as much as a combined one. Who knows, I might go all traditional next time with photo only book but like this it will be limited.

I have often said I consider myself more of a songwriter than a poet but many say I am both and poetry is the artform I neglect most but 2022 saw me embrace the poetry strand of my Geisha lifestyle a lot more. In the past, I may have read one or two poems at one of my photo art exhibitions and the rest found their way into songs. But there have been a few brief highlights in what I would loosely term the poetry department of my life.
The first came when I attended a very bohemian party in the 90s, where everyone was unexpectedly asked to do a turn and showcase a skill. Not having my punk cello in tow or a camera I opted for poetry and because of the way I was dressed and the nature of some poems having erotic words some revellers came up to me calling me Lord Byron reincarnated. Of course, I knew who Lord Byron was but had not read his work but as I was also an adventurer I felt perhaps a kindred spirit lay ahead to discover. However, I got sidetracked and never did another live reading until 2000 which proved very interesting in many ways. I was taking a break from producing music for others, being in a band and running a record label to embark on one of my many adventures. This one involved sticking a pin in a map and following it to Florida in America then opening a local newspaper at a random page upon my arrival and seeing the words Naked Poetry. I knew this was an event I had to be at. Initially, I was happy just to be a spectator lurking in the shadows but naked flesh however was thin on the ground, although a few people did take the event marquee literally. Then I took a shine to what turned out to be another songwriter and poet and after talking with her she challenged me to get up and do a few words. An album by my band of that moment in time, Box Office Poison, had a track on it I had written called 'Sex on the Internet'. It was observational in a Ray Davies sort of way but also humorous and controversial and it went down extremely well like a hooker who loves to swallow.

However, a twist was instore, the female poet I was looking to impress was dragged off by a late arriving boyfriend and another female was now front and centre asking me for an interview after telling me how much she loved my Beatnick delivery. (not that I knew what that was exactly).

It turned out she was the editor of a leading poetry magazine and I was soon back at her place but the passions of the night took over and I don't remember too much about the interview only that I did one and it had gone down well. The full story of this episode will no doubt feature in my autobiography and does feature in my novel 'Adventures of A Dark Duke: The Pin'. (Nothing like basing fiction on real-life experiences.) But this impromptu performance had given me the bug to embrace poetry more and upon my return home I made enquiries about doing some performances at places like The Troubadour in London and others, but they seemed a bit cliquey and being the new kid on the block the welcome sign seemed turned off. Then I encountered the other scourge of the poetry world (Although it also takes place in the other arts) and that was to pay for the privilege of spouting your work via a million and one competitions and even some live events. No, no, no! I had already helped expose scams in the music business via my book Music Business Bastards (How to do well in the Music Business without getting ripped off).

Sadly in all the arts there is more talent than opportunities, so artists get exploited. Some just accept it and are desperate to get their work heard, others find a nasty taste swilling around in their mouth and are desperate to spit it in the face of those doing the exploiting. So, put off by this state of affairs, I carried on with music producing and photography to earn my living and my songs were released regularly worldwide to give those poetic words somewhere to breathe.

My next brush with poetry was in 2005 and was a very pleasant but unexpected one. I have always been sceptical about awards but I do have one for 'International Poem of the Year' '. This came about when a friend of mine sent the lyrics to one of my songs 'Magic', to an international poetry competition. I only heard about it when it won and I got sent the award. My friend said she thought this lyric was as good as, if not much better than any poetry she had read, so had entered it into this competition. So I guess people do rate me as a poet. However, having won an award I thought I would quit while I was ahead and anyway preferred writing songs, so my poetry found its way into many song releases after that. But come 2016 my photography career had gone into overdrive and I felt a book of it was required but rather than just release a photography book I wanted to do something different, so thought I would alternate it with song lyrics but I also had a batch of poetry lying around that hadn't become songs and would prove a rare angle for fans, so 'Voyeurs Welcome Vol.1' was born. It was a limited edition but I decided against convention and made it a quality paperback rather than a traditional hardback. There was, however, a method in my madness in that many of my music fans could afford this format but may struggle to get a very expensive hardback and I wanted it accessible to everybody. The decision paid off as it sold out within 2 weeks of release. Then to my surprise went up in price on the collectors market (Many of my music releases had become collectable and it's definitely a space I like to live in). It has now reached 20 times its original price.

A few years down the line with many photo exhibitions coming up, including my first month long solo one, I decided it was time for Vol.2 and this is just about to sell out. In 2022 after the lockdown, I was invited to many events and for some reason, poetry was part of what was going down. I guess people had a lot of time to collect their thoughts whille confined. While in attendence watching others I was asked perform some poetry as people were aware of the lyrics of my songs and my book. The words went down so well I thought I'd give it a good outing this year. Then at art exhibitions, some artists and customers were moved to tears after leafing through 'Voyeurs Welcome Vol.2' (then buying it), which is the reaction an artist wants at the end of the day, to move and affect people with any art form they do.

Also, if the result ends up feeding the artist as well that's a bonus. People putting their hand in thier pockets is the ultimate review of your works, 'likes' don't really mean anything these days and certainly don't pay the rent.

So with V.W Vol.2 about to sell out and the reaction I was getting lately, this was the catalyst for this poetry-only book. Ironically when the V.W books first came out, although people liked the combination of words & images it was the images that had been getting the wow factor, now all of a sudden the words had overshadowed the images. Also, I got lucky in some sense, in that lyrics I'd written long ago that came out in a previous music release 'More Than the Truth' became a popular favourite with Ukrainians via Spotify as it summed up what they were going through in their country. So, my words never seem to go out of fashion, which adds to proceedings. Long may it continue.

As for the poetry in this book, it is a mixture of observations, message type odes, humour, autobiographical and others that defy category and it's easy to tell the ones that ended up as songs. Ministry of Ska did rude boy humour so that should be taken into consideration when reading those type of poems/lyrics. So don't be put off with what some might consider dark content early on, the book has many shades to offer.

LIFE'S GREAT ADVENTURE

I'd lived my life on the edge more times than I'd care to remember
I am a collector of broken people
Waifs, strays, misfits, people who felt they don't belong

Some illnesses can be fixed by a potion here or remedy there
But hidden illness walks amongst you every day living behind a painted smile
Only on these people the paint never dries

Why did these people always gravitate towards me?
And more importantly why was I drawn to them?
Like a cheap sketch by an unknown artist

Fascination, intrigue, something different to the norm. Yes, sometimes I'm glad I was
born. Like a moth to a flame, sometimes you never get to know their name

It was time for a new adventure and I wondered what cast of characters lay ahead
Every experience in life is like a scar within, multiplying
Until you die the death of thousand paper cuts, it drives you nuts

We all start with a blank slate, so why do some people love and some people hate?
Why do some people love and some people hate?

Rejection and how you handle it, it's your starter for ten and it's your decision as to
whether you ever go there again. So start your adventure and pick up your pen

Of course, every experience creates your character, so there is no escaping it, unless
you want to be as blank as that piece of paper

So you venture out with the best intentions and then innocence meets experience.
Often experience has a chip on its shoulder. Then pretty soon you are taking your first
bite out of life's great potato

Welcome to the world, it's how you deal with it that counts, little things or large
amounts
As I said, I've met a lot of people in my life and I often think, if only I met them before
their last trauma I could have made them feel so much warmer, made them feel
positive about themselves.
But it's often too late and they bring their baggage with them and unluckily for me, I
get to unpack it one item at a time only to find out they shouldn't be mine. So, after a
quick embrace, I pack my case and leave to join the human race, alone again and
just another face.
Yes, how many journeys can you take before you make the same mistake?
Life's for living, it's about give and take. So, who will take and who will give? That's
the game of life that you will learn how to live. Yes, learn how to live.

I WANT TO PAINT IT

Don't you know that life can be so unkind?
Don't you know, it's all about the people left behind?
Walking thru dark alleyways leading the blind
A look over your shoulder will leave you far behind

Dead men's shoes never felt so unkind
They fit so badly that your feet begin to grind
You just want to put your past life behind

I want to paint it
Do you know what pain is?
It's just one less letter to confess
Words of confusion and disillusion that leave you in a mess
I want to paint it
It's pain without a T
It's coming back to me
T stands for trauma

When you're feeling far away
It's just another day
Another chance to say the things you could never say

Walking towards the doorway of a broken mind
You never know what you might find.

I want to paint it
Don't you know what pain is?
It's just one less letter to confess
Words of confusion and disillusion that leave you in a mess
I want to paint it
It's pain without a T
T is for trauma,…that's reality

DANGEROUS GAME

As thoughts turn to past romance, a sexy person and a real slow dance
A strange feeling a certain stance, you think again about a second chance
You're playing a dangerous game, anonymity could change to fame

You're playing a dangerous game

We are who we are we have come too far
To go back would be like crashing in the same old car
You move on for a reason, time to celebrate a new season
Oh, you're playing a dangerous game

Memories can lead to the road of despair
Dwelling in the past leads to love that never lasts
We're playing a dangerous game, obscurity could change to fame
We are all playing a dangerous game.

Look, look, look.. pictures in a book
Who is it that took took took
Rose-tinted glasses are worn by asses

Oh you're playing a dangerous game

As thoughts turn to past romance, a sexy person a real slow dance
A strange feeling a certain stance, you think again about a second chance

You're playing a dangerous game, that could hurt or maim
Oh you're playing a dangerous game
Playing a dangerous game that could hurt or maim
Oh we're all playing a dangerous game
A dangerous game

Always think twice, unless you enjoy pain
Or you're likely to go insane
That's why it's a dangerous game

NUMBERS

From when you are born to when you die
You are just a number no matter how hard you try
From D.O.B to R.I.P is that really me?

From your living zone to your telephone
From the plate on your car or entry to a bar
Is that really me?

Numbers, numbers, don't judge me..don't judge me
Numbers, numbers, don't judge me
I have more to offer than mediocrity
Numbers, numbers, don't judge me
Does it really tell you what you see?

See a number next to a name
Does it really mean that we're all the same
Too young, too old, too warm to cold
I'm not a sheep waiting to be told
What is the price of gold

Numbers, numbers, don't judge me..don't judge me
Numbers, numbers, don't judge me
I have more to offer than mediocrity
Numbers, numbers, don't judge me
Does it really tell you what you see
Numbers. numbers can't you see
Never settle for mediocrity

12345678 don't be late.

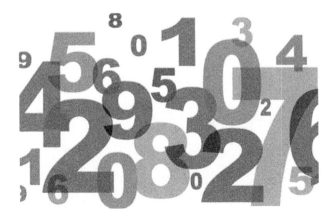

MAGIC

When the night takes your mind away and teaches it new tricks to play
And your soul begins to glide and shows you pictures from the other side

Dust the cobwebs from your soul and you start to search as it takes hold
When the night takes your mind away and teaches it new tricks to play
And your soul begins to glide and shows you pictures from the other side

The shadow gangsters have come to take control
The shadow gangsters have come to take control

Feel those hands so deep inside holding back the darkest tide like magic
It's like magic, it's magic

Let time lick your wounds away, try to keep the pain at bay
Time to put those memories away
Time to put those memories away

Feel those hands so deep inside holding back that scary ride like magic
It's like magic, it's magic

You look but you do not see

You listen but you do not hear

You touch but you do not feel

Oh, are you real

Oh, are you real

Are you real

BACKSTREET BOULEVARD

Stroll on, stroll on down the street
Electricity flows through your feet
Down and outs are all you meet
Huddled together for body heat

You've got to be so hard
On backstreet boulevard
All weakness is barred
On backstreet boulevard

My god love, you look a terrible sight
So would you, if you'd been open all night

Junkie, flunkie, why take dope?
Because without it there's no hope

You've got to be so hard
On backstreet boulevard
All weakness is barred
On backstreet boulevard

Junkies, wino's, pimps and hookers
You're nothing to them except onlookers
They crave and kroner, ten pence or a dime
The outstretched hand is the same world mime

You've got to be so hard, You got to be so hard
On backstreet boulevard

ARTISTIC SOULMATES

She's here, she's here
She came to me through the splash of an Angels tear

When love is not enough and the going gets tough
You need a soulmate. We never hesitate
We always celebrate, that we are soulmates

We take a ride, one on one
Our journey has begun
It's an artistic vibe
It makes us and our work come alive
Pushing the boundaries we always thrive

Never will we witness another grey day
Because we are moulded from the same artistic clay
A clay to play with and show us the way
Because we are soulmates forever and a day
Really soulmates

When our souls begin to glide
We feel each other deep inside
Together it's a feeling we can never hide
It always makes us come alive so very deep inside

When I die I want to float away
But I need to kiss her every day
Soulmates in every way
We'll meet again in a different way
Because we are forever artistic soulmates

WELCOME TO THE BUREAU OF AFFECTION

We are all analogue people living in a digital world!

Why is it that when you love someone they don't love you
Or when someone loves you, you don't love them
Then you hear that dreaded phrase, let's just be friends
It's enough to drive you around the bend.

Welcome to the Affection Bureau,
Welcome to the Bureau of Affection
Look out it's coming in your direction,
Looking to make the ultimate connection
I'm hoping to find it at the Bureau of Affection.

Dating on the internet can be a losing bet
A trunk full of trauma is all you'll get
But I'll keep on trying, I'm not dead yet
Some you win and some you regret

We are all analogue people living in a digital world
Android sheep controlled by apps
Living our lives through second-hand vibes
Through mobile technology, part of robot tribes.

Welcome to the Affection Bureau.
Welcome to the Bureau of Affection
Look out it's coming in your direction.
Looking to make the ultimate connection
I'm hoping to find it at the Bureau of Affection

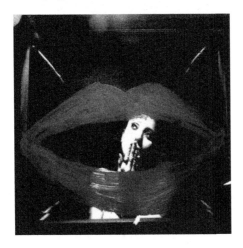

IS IT PASSION THAT YOU FEEL?

I see a reflection of myself in your eyes
I guess it should come as no surprise
I live on through the same disguise
I was dumb but now I'm wise

Sing a song of a twisted tale
Crimes of passion don't need no bail
Successful stories of people who fail
French letters delivered by male

Is this passion that I feel
Is this passion really real
Passion is for lovers
Who hide under the covers
I love passion, I love passion
Tell me it's passion that you feel?

I smell and feel erotic sweat on your cheek
Is it part of the love that you seek?
The knots in your hair help secure the affair
Tying you up and keeping you there

A while ago you were just a glance
But now you've taken my poor heart by chance
Set me free and let's dance
This could be a big romance

Is this passion for real
Yes, it's passion that I feel
Shall we run for cover
Or will you be my lover
Is this passion very real
Yes, it's the real deal
I love passion, I love passion

DON'T SHUT YOUR MOUTH

I am the sun and the air of a planet that has been criminally broken
I am the son and heir of nowhere anymore

So, shut your mouth, don't steal my air, it's not fair
Am I not human?
No, but I'm trying to survive
Just like this planet is

I am the moon and the water
The planet is my adopted daughter
You rape her at your peril

So, don't shut your mouth,
Speak out and make a difference

So, it's time to do something, but what can you do?
You're all alone in a new wasteland

The time is now, don't hesitate, it's not too late

We have already waited too long
and now my hope is fading and life is trading in on itself

I am the fire and the earth that has lost its worth
I am the earth and fire walking a tight rope wire

A silent mouth, a star goes out
The sky is dark. Who has left their mark?

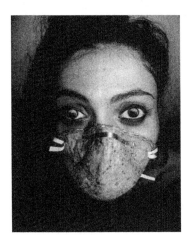

MORE THAN THE TRUTH

Why do you do what you do?
Does power entertain you?
More than the truth
Yeah, more than the truth

You invaded our culture
You invaded our minds
We didn't want you
No, we didn't want you

You think you're an ace
But your just a disgrace
You're just a cheat
A dirty old cheat. Yeah

But now we're out to get you
You've stepped on too many toes
You should have kept your mouth shut
And blew your brains right out of your nose

Why do you do what you do?
Does power entertain you?
More than the truth. Yeah, more than the truth

Lies were his game
He just wanted fame
But nobody knew, no, nobody knew

He has an accent and a pension book to
Do you know who he is?
I think you know who he is?
More than the truth. Yeah, more than the truth

THINK FOR YOURSELF

What are we here for? What's it all about?
Who are we bluffing? I want to scream and shout
Cigarette perfume litters your breath
Time to get going, to the house on the corner
Drink yourself to death

Think for yourself don't be a fool
Think for yourself you can be cool
Think for yourself, think for yourself

Living in a catalogue world
Buy and sell your life
Unfaithful husbands looking for someone else's wife
Adverts sound as sweet as honey
But all the really want is your money

So no to people ruling your life
From when you're a daughter to when you're a wife
Stay individual and do what is right

Think for yourself don't be a fool
Think for yourself you can be cool
Think for yourself, think for yourself

FEMME FATALE

Hello, I'm a Femme Fatale, listen up, I've got a story to tell
Hello, I'm a Femme Fatale, lock up your heart, I'm about to send it to hell

I will always treat you like dirt, being with me will always hurt
But even the dirt you taste will make you feel alive, part of the human race
Of me, you can never get enough, no matter how many times you call my bluff

I'll send you away feeling sore, yes it's you that's my little whore
But time and again you'll come back for more.

Listen up, I'm a Femme Fatale. I like a bad boy
They always use me like a toy
But our passion is the real Mcoy

To die together is our destiny, it's the only end for you and me
But for now, we need a patsy to drive around the bend
He will think it's love in bloom
But all he'll get is a gas chamber fume

Look around any corner you will find a sap
Whose destiny is to always take the rap

I'm a Femme Fatale and I take no crap
That's my story welcome to my trap.

(Half a girl is better than none, but one crazy girl is no fun
I'm feeling the weight of a gun, now it's time to go on the run
No fun, no fun, no fun, I'm done)

CELLO IN MY SOUL

Through early morning mist I see bloodshot eyes staring back at me
Desperately begging for a cup of tea. One small kiss would set me free

The Cello was playing in my soul
My spirit reaching its goal
She was the Cello in my soul
The strings were taking their toll
She was the Cello in my soul, Cello in my soul

Night turned to day and her mind begin to play
Desperately searching for a catchy phrase
Music inspired from a drunken haze
She was going through a creative phase
Her mind was brilliant but often like a maze

Sometimes it seemed like there was no way out
So she would just scream and shout
But eventually, a nice little tune would spring right out
But what were those lyrics all about?

Cello in my soul. The strings are taking their toll
Cello in my soul. The sounds are out of control
Because the Cellos in my soul. She was the cello in my soul

Together or apart we were a work of art
A living, breathing connection right from the start
Cut short in our prime before our time
But our legacy lives on, even now we are gone

She went off to Camden town with her knickers hanging down
With her ankles well and truly bent, she began giving vent
Her waterworks now translated from her misspent rent
After a night in the pub that she would often frequent

But she will forever be the Cello in my soul

ONE WAY TICKET TO THE MOON

My head is spinnining. I can't stop winning
Heart and soul, I can't control

Pieces of me everywhere, floating through exotic air
Land to Land … hand to hand

Girl in every port

Emotions sold and bought
Hooked on foreign export
It's multiple love that I have to report

I need a one-way ticket to the moon
I want to hear a melody to a different tune
I need a one-way ticket to the moon
Another blind date behind a windswept dune

It's driving me crazy I can't choose
It's a feeling I just don't want to lose

A girl in every port, erotic export
A girl in every port, sexual import

I need a one-way ticket to the moon
Let me hear a melody to a different tune
I need a one-way ticket to the moon
Another blind date behind a windswept dune

A CONGA THRU HISTORY

She could conga for Britain
Once shy twice bitten
A brush with fame
In a faded picture frame

The nearly model of the catwalk twirl
A society bunch living in a whirl
She was looking for a prince but found an earl
He was looking to pollinate her pearl
And we all know what happened when you use a girl

But the seaside tower
Is where she would grow her flower
Not the tower in France
Indiscretion saw her miss her big chance

Balmain was her second shot at fame
But then her lungs began to inflame
Leading to a proposal that would change her name
But her life would never be the same

The postcard appeal would see her become the real deal
World famous at last amongst a collectors class
She had stepped thru the looking glass

A conga thru history revealed many a mystery
Mystery, mystery, mystery
It turned out we all had a different history

(F o r   M u m)

IT IS WHAT IT IS

From SR4 to my front door
Love lies bleeding on the floor
Murdered before it began
Yes, murdered before it began

Two scared hearts that couldn't say
I can, I can, I can, I can

It is what it is, what it is, what it is, what it is
Yes, it is what it is, what it is, what it is, what it is
Hit and miss, hit and miss, hit and miss, hit and miss
Because it is what it is, what it is, what it is, what it is
The bliss of a kiss of a kiss, of a kiss of a kiss, of a kiss of a kiss
Because it is what it is, what it is, what it is, what it is

A cold wind blows down the Holloway Road
The ghosts were calling, the wild wind was blowing
But there was no way that I'd see you going

It is what it is, what it is, what it is, what it is
Hit and miss. The bliss of a kiss
It is what it is, what it is, what it is, what it is

Another Sunday horoscope
Two hearts beat with hope
Another chance to share the soap
Two entities trying to cope

It is what it is, what it is, what it is, what it is

CRY OUT THE PAIN

A wedding ring in a bottom draw, two cold hearts that beat no more
Passion reels at the thought of pain, it's back in town again

You shook my confidence and made me feel low
Life has no meaning with nowhere to go
A breathless body lies on the floor
Just one more soul who couldn't take anymore

I wish I could cry out the pain
Because I never want to feel it again
I wish I could cry out the pain
No, I never want to see you again

I'll eat my heart out if there's a shadow of doubt
And sell my soul to the devil's tout
To put my heart on the line
And stop this, this decline

I wish I could cry out the pain
Because I never want to feel it again
I wish I could cry out the pain
No, I never want to see you again

Crying, crying, crying

Out the pain

The pain

SEX ON THE INTERNET

Sexy girl seeks sexy boy, sexy boy seeks sexy girl
Purpose......... Swap fantasies
Sexy boy meets sexy girl, sexy girl meets sexy boy
Purpose.......Danger with a stranger

Sex on the Internet. It keeps you warm it keeps you wet
Sex on the Internet. It's up to you what you get

Cyber-girl seeks cyber-boy, cyber-boy seeks cyber-girl
Purpose.........Cyber-sex

Sex on the internet, sex on the internet

Submit here have no fear
You're so far and yet so near
Sex on the Internet, sex on the Internet

Boy seeks boy, girl seeks girl
The internet is a different world
Purpose....To be somebody else

Sex on the Internet
I want it here, I want it now!
Sex on the Internet. Watch out girls here it comes
Sex on the Internet. Wipe the screen and keep it clean

E-mail me your ultimate fantasy
Don't hold back, don't keep it clean
Swap sexy photos over the net
It's an experience you won't forget
We are all voyeurs. We just don't like to admit it
We're all voyeurs. We're all in it

IS IT SEX YOU SEEK

I could be in Casablanca, romance dripping from the wall
But now I'm on the streets of Soho and I'm the one you call
One thing I've learnt in this life
There's no luck for me at all

Is it sex you seek?
Or just a peak of my body writhing
Is it sex you seek?
Your flesh is weak
See my mind dividing
Is it sex you seek?
Let me hear you speak
Your words of lying

Is it sex you seek?
This old body's weak
From its daily pounding
Is it sex you seek?
My whole life is bleak from my surroundings
Is it sex you seek?
Hear my body creak
Please stop this hounding!

SEXUAL GIRL

The breath from her body blew me away
The wink from her eye told me it was time to play
Her lip stained lips and her sensual hips
Couldn't wait to get my mouth around her nips

Sexual girl, sexual girl

Sexual girl, sexual girl, give me a whirl

Sexual boy, sexual boy, I'm not your toy
I'm not just here for you to enjoy
My emotions need to employ
A degree of intelligence will bring you Joy
Then I will play and make your day

People are more the looks, why don't you read some books

Your natural desire with get you higher
But in the end you will burn like fire

Sexual boy, sexual boy

I WANT YOU ALL THE TIME

Fatal attraction, physical attraction, explosive action
Chemical reaction, intelligent retraction, more and more action
That's us, that's us

I want you, I want you, I want you, I want you, I want you all the time
Every day and every night
I want you, I want, I want you, I want you all the time
I want you, I want you, I want you, I want you, want you all my life

A sudden movement, a certain look
His body froze and then it shook
He opened me up like a book, a passionate chapter, then the hook

Possession is aggression
Obsession is regression

I want you, I want you, I want you, I want you, I want you all the time
I want you, I want you, I want you, I want you, want you all the time

Possession is aggression
Obsession is regression
Kiss goodbye to your mind

I want you, I want you, I want you, I want you, I want you all the time
I want you, I want you, I want you, I want you all my life
I want you ...I want you

Surfing on the seedy side. It's something that I can't hide
I slip and I slide but I always enjoy the ride
You'll always be part of me

COME WITH ME

Come, come, come with me
To an island inside of me
Oh, I'm breathing heavily
Cum with me

The night is young but can't you see
I just want you inside of me
Let me feel you inside of me
Set me free

Whispers of love pass to and fro
Feel my body and then let go
Oh, this feeling I can't control
Cum with me

How I wish you could only see how much pleasure you are giving me
Oh, touch me, touch me there. Set me free

Our bodies tense and our spirits flow
I wish this feeling could never go
Oh it's special with you. Cum with me

Come, come, come with me
To an island inside of me
Oh, I'm breathing heavily. Cum with me

Come, come, come with me. To an island inside of me, inside of me
I can't control this! I can't control this!
Cum with me!

EROTIC BLOOD

An early morning light ushers in a wonderful sight
A perfect dawn gives birth to the silhouette of a female form

When a sexy girl stands naked in front of you with their legs closed often there is a
small gap between the upper thighs and just below the virgina and it creates a heart
shape, it's then I know it's a sign that I'm in love

Yes, I'm the man who drips erotic blood

A sensual horse grabs the reigns and charges through my blood-soaked veins
Pumping, pulsing, looking for some sexual rain

Yes, I'm the man with erotic blood

They say if I bled I would bleed erotic blood. It never stops giving and creates a flood

Drip drip drip on a nip, flowing fast towards a clit

I'm the man that bleeds erotic blood

It's a feeling I wear like an exotic glove
It's a tight fit, a beautiful clit
To observe is my only remit
To worship at the altar of life's great slit

Yes, I'm the man who bleeds erotic blood it keeps on flowing,
growing and soon it will be glowing.
Soon to pour onto a bedroom floor until I can't give anymore
It's a homage to more and more.
Just a metaphor for how it feels to have erotic blood

My lines are sensual, they say it gets them wet
Hold on just a minute, you ain't seen nothing yet

TOO SAD TO CRY

Just a tear-stained face on a pillowcase
Liquids of heartbreak that leave no trace
Hold out a hand for a loving embrace
Life can be such a cruel place

I'm too sad to cry…Too sad to cry
But I don't know why, no, I don't know why
I'm too sad to cry…Too sad to cry but I don't know why

Too personal to tell of my living hell
Too hurt to yell…Oh well, oh well, oh well

I can't shed a tear for you my dear
It's only been a week but it feels like a year
I don't want to see you but I wish you were near
I would change everything just to have you here

I'm too sad to cry…too sad to cry
But I don't know why, no I don't know why
I'm too sad to cry…Too sad to cry but I don't know why

SEA OF SOULS

It's a crazy messed up kinda shit
When you have to kill someone because they have a clit

Millions of souls floating over China
Who died and died just because they owned a vagina

Surfing on the sea of souls,
Waves and waves, that never grow old
No affection it feels so cold, sea of souls
Sea of souls, sea of souls, sea of souls, sea of souls
Crying out to reach their goals
Empty life's living full of holes

Exposure is here, karma has arrived
The powerful are tumbling where they once had thrived
Politicians with their hand in the till
It's enough to make you ill, ill, ill, ill

From the press barons to the incompetent shower
Who get paid for failure hour upon hour
Police corruption is causing an eruption
More and more people looking for destruction

Surfing on the sea of souls
Waves and waves of forgotten souls
Trampled over by those with hidden goals

Surfing on the sea of souls .....it's so sad, it fills me full of holes.
Sea of souls, sea of souls, sea of souls, sea of souls, sea of souls
Justice is near, so never fear, don't hold it inside and shed that tear

PSYCHIC HOLIDAY

There's an Alien in my living room and spunk stains on my bed
I've only been home half an hour and someone's playing with my head

I hear a click on my phone, now I know I'm not alone
When my home is just one big…. listening zone

It's nearly 23 hundred hours ….my clock is tick tick ticking
My mind has been overrun and now its stick, stick sticking
This paranoia ………needs lick, lick licking
Am I the one to give it a kick, kick, kicking

I need a psychic holiday, a place where bad vibes go away
I need a psychic holiday, somewhere to keep the world at bay, psychic, psychic,
holiday, I need a psychic holiday,
Yes, I need a psychic holiday; I need a psychic holiday

There's a shadow in the doorway
Footsteps in my ears
My journey was but a moment
But symptoms last for years

Ten thousand downloads from the Internet
From people that I've never met
Now I'm living in a doorway
All because I never got paid

I need a psychic…psychic….I need a psychic holiday
Where my mind shines every day
I need a psychic holiday, somewhere to keep the world at bay
I need a psychic holiday, a place where bad vibes go away
I need a psychic holiday

LAST GEISHA STANDING

With your Anthony Newly voice and your life so full of choice
So many labels put you in their stables
But it was you who turned the tables

Mistakes were made but a least you played and got well laid
But along came a hero from outta space
To help you win that elusive chart race
No longer stuck in a can
Your career just ran and ran

The Starman said it was time to go
Now it's up to you to finish the show
A photograph casts a ghostly glow
But now it's time for me to grow

I'm the last Geisha standing. Look out earth I'm landing
I'm the last Geisha standing. Understanding my branding
I'm the last Geisha standing, so alone, not a clone
So far away from my natural home.

The Stargirl held out her hand
To take you to a foreign land
To expand your creative gland
To escape a world that has become so bland

There's a star girl shining in the sky
And only I know why, yes only I know why
There's a Stargirl shining in the sky
She needs a human guy
There's a Stargirl in the sky
And she wants someone with a different eye
So now it's time to fly. Stargirl, Stargirl

HOW DO YOU SLEEP

A crumpled suit with a frayed lapel
Bug-repellent wafts through a cheap hotel
He screams inside but you can't hear him yell
Each grey hair has a different story to tell

How do you sleep...How do you sleep
Have you forgotten how to weep
Moments fade but thoughts run deep
Must we all behave like sheep
Who shall sow and who shall reap
How do you sleep how do you sleep?

You pass them every day of your life
It could have been you, it could have been your wife

Spare a thought for the ten-cent life....Spare a thought for the ten-cent life

How do you sleep...How do you sleep?
Have you forgotten how to weep
Moments fade but thoughts run deep
Must we all behave like sheep
If you sow who shall reap
How do you sleep how do you sleep?

The damp on the wall was there to remind him of nothing at all
The sum total of the achievements of his life
He was surrounded by second-hand brick a brac
That once belonged to someone who died of a heart attack
He himself had one sock in the grave
But the way out sign found him feeling brave

LOCKDOWN

How many alcoholics must we create?
How many relationships will turn to hate?
How many children will melt & break?
How many heroes did we kill by mistake?

Lock, lock, lockdown

In an empty town
The angel of death has lost his frown
The whole planet is down down down
The grim reaper has regained his crown

Lock, lock, lockdown

Our sense of freedom has gone underground
We are all slowing down
Soon we will feel like we want to drown
A fashion statement is now a dressing gown

The people in charge are living it large
Greasy palms with outstretched arms
Wearing a disguise, never to apologise
We will never forget you owe us a debt

Why did the rich and famous never die
Was it down to old school tie?
One thing's for sure they know how to lie
Now it's time for the clown's goodbye

But nobody is laughing anymore
But at least those left can step through the door
Only to introduce a new dilemma to keep us poor
And if that's not enough we will give you a war

DEATH DECADE

The decade of death has drawn its last breath
The decade of death has left us bereft
Of those we love but will never forget

When you are cut from the womb
Your life begins to zoom
Ups and downs, different cities, different towns
But there are always special people around
Family ties that keep us bound

When your loved ones depart
You are never really apart
Because they colour your life
Like a work of art
Protecting you from the other side
Always playing their part

DON'T TOUCH MY BIKINI

Woke up this morning with the hump
Needed to make use of this bump
Went in search of some camel toe
Swinging in my boxers to and fro

Sauntered along to the beach
Looking for a lovely peach
Rub sun cream on her back
Then later on jump in the sack

Don't touch my bikini
Those were the only words I heard
My god, she was such a fuzzy bird
Don't touch my bikini, don't touch my bikini
Don't touch my bikini, don't touch my bikini

So there I was in bikini paradise
Nice little cocktail filled with ice
Sun-tanned bodies looking very nice
I gave it another go and threw the dice

Don't touch my bikini. She said it to me twice
So instead of sun-cream, I covered her with ice

Don't touch my bikini she slapped me in the face
Don't touch my bikini or I'll kick you in a place
Where your hump will slump and your balls will jump
Don't touch my bikini but touch the rest of me
Can't you see my camel toe needs rubbing to bring me ecstasy?

Soon enough she had no bikini
So I drank her Bellini and it tasted very creamy...And so did I

NORMAN

Norman was the straightest guy
He was as narrow as his tie
His glasses had a horny rim
Because he knew they suited him

His suits never fitted him well
Made him look like a liberty bell
Norman's hair was greasy and grey
Until Chicken Licken took it away

Oh, Norman you're so tasty
You've got a face like puffed up pastry
Why do all the girls fancy you? Is it right are the rumours true?

Is it true that the things in your brain
Are so boring they give you a pain?
Oh, Norman you must have a shave
We don't like to see your whiskers wave

Oh, Norman you're one of the pinstripe
Oh, Norman you're one of the pinstripe brigade
But you dream about the day you get paid
And about the Smurf that you laid

Oh, Norman you're so tasty
You've got a face like puffed up pastry
Why do all the girls fancy you? Is it right are the rumours true?

I remember the day I heard Norman scream
As he drowned in a bottle of his own Brill Cream
The only sight left to be seen
Were Norman's horn rims in a cloud of steam

CONDOM

Hey Errol, me want some pussy push-ups tonight

When I was a little boy, me had a favourite toy
It was a white balloon but when I came it was too soon
Pretty soon I was a man and met a girl called Pam
I want to spunk up all night but she put up a terrible fight

The only thing she said to me was....... condom
Where's your condom
You must have a condom
Where's your condom
Me want condom. Ooh condom

I & I on another day, looked for pussy that wanted to play
Doris was the girl that I found, but she looked like Huckleberry Hound

Me no want baby look like, that. She looks so ugly it looks so fat
But the only thing upon her mind was to grab me and give me a ...grind.

Me want condom, me want condom. Where's my condom? CCCCC condom
What's it called now? Oh yeah condom
Me want condom...I need a condom

Hey, pass the vaseline Doris
Give me that packet of three now
Hey Errol is this the 12" version
If it is all the ladies like a 12" version
The only trouble is you can't get a condom to fit 12"
And I should know.
condom, oh condom.

I WANT TO SLEEP WITH YOU (PT.2)

She starts her day the feminine way, ooh dressed to kill
She turns on the T.V set and it says sex will make you ill
She remembers a time when it was such a thrill
That was so long ago. It just goes to show
But she can't say no

She can't help herself, she just wants to sleep with you
L.O.V.E her and she will love you to
She can't help herself, she just wants to sleep with you
L.O.V.E her and she will love you to

Open up the paper, another victim to depress
Love or joy, oh boy, her life is such a mess
You see she's not a loose girl, she just loves to love
She has seen the figures. She knows the risks
But it's such a test

Love or lust at first sight always turns her on
She's sexually attracted, but it's really love that she wants
But now her mans been unfaithful and it starts to show
His HIV test no longer says no
It's a shattering blow

She doesn't want to sleep with you
It's too late and now she is a victim too
She never wants to sleep with you
It's too late and now her life is forever blue

ALIEN

Alien, oh Alien. Save me tonight
Alien, Alien. Come take a flight
Alien, oh Alien. Save us from our plight

Alien, sweet Alien. Come save us tonight
Alien, sweet Alien. Come take a flight

Alien, sweet Alien
Come and save us from ourselves

The planet's in a mess
People are in distress
It's time to address the problems that we face

Alien, oh Alien. Come save me tonight
Alien, oh Alien. I won't put up a fight.
Alien, sweet Alien. Make everything all right

You haven't lived till you've made love to an Alien
Your senses expand and you cum and cum, with an Alien
This is the ultimate one on one, with an Alien

Alien, Alien, Alien, Alien, Alien, Alien

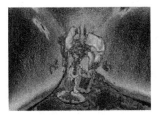

NEXT TIME

They say if you could change your life, would you?
They say if you could go back in time and change anything would you
People usually say no but I say let's go

I'll get it right in the next life
I'll get it right with a new wife
Yes, I'll get it right in the next life
Let me go and join my new wife

People often say they wouldn't change a thing
As for me, I'm changing everything
Life is like a karmic tool
But I never want to play the fool

Sometimes I sit here and fantazise
That I'll find someone who won't criticise
Someone oh so wise
Try me out, I'm just your size

I thought you were someone special, sorry my mistake
At least you've saved me years of heartbreak

So many people pretending to be in love
So as not to be alone
But alone you can face your true zone
What you really need is a clone

SUMMER OF 42 REVISITED

She looked like Glenda Jackson and we certainly saw some action
She could have been my mum but age is just a sum
I loved the way she moved and together we just grooved
But my mother always disapproved

Age has no meaning when your teenage hormones are teeming
Every night I'd go to sleep dreaming, that this romance had some meaning
Age has no meaning when your teenage hormones are streaming
Every night I'd go to sleep with the look on her face still gleaming

We all need a summer of 42, let me tell you it's so good for you
Memories are just like glue, they stick with you
We all need a summer of 42. We're all young once and need a clue
Experience is crucial and she was my summer of 42

Forget summer the first time, it was summer the second time that was mine
A repeat performance with different feline
Only this time the purring was mutual
No longer the awkward teenager but there was still a gap but I didn't need a map

A second summer came around for me,
As the world experienced its biggest catastrophe
She came in a shapely tight business suit. She was so fine and an upper-class beaut
I was older now but this one liked a row but her experience just made me go wow
She was there for me throughout a world of mediocrity
The dark horse and the gem sparkling together as they felt so free

We all need a summer of 42, let me tell you it's so good for you
Memories are just like glue, they stick with you
We all need a summer of 42, forget just once your need a few
All experiences are crucial and she was my next summer of 42

Finally, I look back on my life and I had 42 summers to remember
whilst hibernating every November
Every one a time to savour with a different flavour
Was I a tart with a heart or just a sex-mad person captured by art
You've got to live life and experience everything
That's the only consolation if you never wear the ring
Passion is on ration with a world built on fashion
As long as it's a two-way street you are never short on action
So enjoy your summer of 42 and I'll be thinking of you.

A SCRIPTED AFFAIR

The Count is in the corner counting out his kisses
The females around the table are writing out their wishes
Diana is quietly admiring her own breast
But Gary's bloodshot eyes just haven't passed the test

It's a scripted affair, a media dare, breathing celebrity air
Yes it's a scripted affair, written by hacks that have no flair
When sincerity is rare there are no souls to bare
It's a scripted affair even though nobody's there

The money men are all in a huddle
But nobody there will give them a cuddle
Because their facts and figures are such a muddle
They will tax your brain and squeeze your tears into a puddle

A famous actor, a famous son, it's a life that's come undone
A city gent seeking rent from a fortune that has been misspent
An ageing actress that is holding back the tide
But people know her far and wide
But if you ask nicely you can come inside
Her experience will leave you with nowhere to hide

It's a scripted affair, a media dare, breathing celebrity air
Yes it's a scripted affair, written by hacks that have no flair
When sincerity is rare there are no souls to bare
It's and scripted affair even though nobody's there

The class of 15 is on its way, on its way to judgement day
Don't you wish you had written that play?
It's the cream of the crop that will shine today with one big ray
All the rest will go away, go away, go away, away

WE'RE ALL INSANE

If love is the answer
The question is a dancer
That tangos with your mind
And grabs you from behind

We're all insane.........we're all insane

You scare me with your problems
Destroy me with your lies
You scar me with your cheating
You're the lover I despise

You're all insane........you're all insane
We're all insane.........we're all insane

Win me today
Lose me tomorrow
You're the creator of your own sorrow

We're all insane.........We're all insane
So insane......................so insane

You threw my flowers down the wishing well
You gave me love but you gave me hell
You threw my flowers down the wishing well

TONIGHT I NEED A KLONE

Tonight I need a Klone. Tonight I need a Klone
Tonight I need a Klone. Tonight I'm all alone
Tonight I need a Klone. I don't want to be on my own

Tonight I need a Klone to know I'm not alone
Tonight I need a Klone to join me in my home

Two rings on my phone. Twins in a multiple zone
Tonight I need a Klone

Someone's ringing my phone
Hello, this is your Klone…I'm lost in a multiple zone
Now I need my Klone. I'm lost in my multiple zone

Tonight I need a Klone. Tonight I need a Klone
I need, I need, I need
To know I'm not alone.
Tonight I need a Klone. Tonight I need a Klone

Living in the moment, I've got too much to do
I am me and you are you
Sometimes I need to split into two, I need a Klone
Yes I need a Klone , yes I need a Klone, yes I need a Klone

MOD GIRLS

Out on the street don't like what I see
Always around don't know who to be
I'm just a girl who needs a boy
What can I do I'm not a toy
See a face who can it be?
I like him. Will he like me?

Mod girls can't be beat, Mod girls are real neat
Mod girls can't be beat, Mod girls are real neat

Where has all the style gone today?
Cool fashion belonged to yesterday
Mini skirts worn by flirts
Handsome blokes in mohair suits
Take my scooter down the coast
Swing with the crowd I like most

Mod girls can't be beat. Mod girls are real neat

Oh, I was born in the wrong age
I want to disappear on a history page
Because the sixties was the place to show your face
Oh, life was forever and always full of grace
Oh, I was born in the wrong time and place

Mod girls can't be beat. Mod girls are real neat

16 YEAR OLD

In the mind of a sixteen year old
The world outside must seem so cold
In the mind of a sixteen year old
Life is about being told. Don't do this, don't do that
You are just a silly brat

Welcome to the world - is it what you thought?
People running around being sold and bought

Welcome to the world -
Is it what you thought it would be?
Is it what you thought it would be?

Life is mixed up for a sixteen year old
No sex - or death, is what you're told
Life is mixed up for a sixteen year old
Politics or money represents your goal

Be in by ten, I won't tell you again
Friction is rife at this time of life

Welcome to the world - is it what you thought?
People running around being sold and bought

Welcome to the world -
Is it what you thought it would be?
Is it what you thought it would be?
Is it what you thought it would be?

ALL I WANT'S A BABY

A life of strife
A downtrodden wife
That life's not for me
I just want to be free

All I want's a baby. Yeah, all I want's a baby

He looked good
I hoped he would
He was six foot three and he fancied me

But all I want's a baby
Baby, Baby, Baby

I got him home to my sexual zone
The passion was right all through the night

Now all I want's a baby
Now all I want's a baby
All I want's a baby

She was born and he never knew
And that's just the way I wanted it too

Now I've got a baby
Yeah now I've got a baby

Baby, baby, baby

NIGHTMARES

Nick knack paddy whack, Freddie's back, Freddie's back

Creeping thru the twilight hours
Drifting through the morning showers
I will see you in your nightmares
In your nightmares
In your nightmares

I will steal your mind in the blackness of night
And send you images that will give you a fright
I will leave you sweating in the cold light of day
About lots of little demons waiting to take you away

I will see you in your nightmares
In your nightmares
In your nightmares

Skulking around the corners of your deepest fears
I will be within you for years and years

I will see you in your nightmares
In your nightmares
In your nightmares

2025

It was a violent country when the ice age came
The war was over but the world was the same
The eyes were upon us in search of a name
Nothing was answered and the questions remain

Will anyone survive in 25, in 2025
Anyone alive in 25 in 2025

The blackness erupted from the burning snow
The people were running but with nowhere to go
The heat came down like a sledgehammer blow
It happened so fast and I was too slow

Will anyone survive in 25, in 2025
Anyone alive in 25, in 2025
Will anyone survive in 25, in 2025
Anyone alive in 25, in 2025

The sky cleared of mist all around
The sea was frozen and as hard as the ground
We lay for a moment void of all sound
The world was in fragments where it once had been round

Will anyone survive in 25, in 2025. Anyone alive in 25 in 2025
Will anyone survive in 25, in 2025. Anyone alive in 25 in 2025

Now we're into atomic override. Who wants to be a radiation bride?

AGENT-M

Tokyo, oh Tokyo...here I go to Tokyo

She takes the train in the morning rain
She can't take the pain and she feels the strain
In Tokyo, in Tokyo...oo oh Tokyo

Don't be sad, don't feel bad
About the life that you've never had
In Tokyo, Tokyo

Life can be bright like a neon light
You've just got to fight and punch above your height
In Tokyo, Tokyo

Close your eyes and pick a disguise................

Agent-M, agent-M, agent-M

There's a spy in my eye and I don't know why
It makes me feel high but I don't want to die
Because I'm agent-M agent-M agent-M
The best spy that you'll ever send
Because I'm agent-M agent-M
The best spy that you'll ever send
The best spy until the end

PSYCHO CITY

I don't much like the look of this place
It looks to me like an ultra rat race
Stress and strain on everyone's face
Everyone looks like a future nutcase

Down in the city when the sun goes down
Scores of villains swarm into town
Someone should have told you not to walk around
Those villains will get you and they won't make a sound

No, you'll get no pity when you visit Psycho city
Psycho; Psycho city, no you'll get no pity
Psycho, Psycho city

Keep your wits about you if you want to survive
Because that's the only way you'll stay alive
Keep locked up safe inside and don't go out after five
Cause that's when the villains thrive

Remember all the things that I have said
And always keep your head
Or you'll wind up stone cold dead
In some dark alley with a belly full of lead

No, you'll get no pity when you visit Psycho city
Psycho, Psycho city, no you'll get no pity
Psycho, Psycho city
Psycho, Psycho city

MYSTERIES

Higher................higher and higher
Let me take you higher
Dream, dream of me
I'm in your head, I'm in your head
No, you're not dead. You're not dead
I'm in your head

Mysteries of the world unite
Now and forever let's take flight
Hanging heavy on your eyelids
Floating thru' the pyramids

Open up your mind and you will find
A different kind
Hello mystery, hello dream
Now you can see me, but do not scream

No! Do not scream
I'm in your dream. I'm in your dream
I am in your head
I'm in your bed. Yes I'm in your bed
Mystery, oh mystery
Mystery, you're my history

Time hangs so heavy on your eyelids. On your eyelids
Now, you're floating thru', floating thru' the Pyramids
Open up your mind and you will find that you're not blind
Oh mystery, mystery, don't you agree, we make a good team

Now your time has come. Don't be scared. Do not run
Now your time has come. Don't be scared. Do not run

GETTING THRU THE DAY

Pushed around from pillar to post
I don't know who I hate the most
Social Security to housing benefit
It's enough to make you sick, sick, sick

I'm just getting thru the day
Won't someone hear a word I say?
I'm just getting thru the day
Hope that things will go my way

Waiting for my money to arrive
No one cares if I survive
The landlord comes and I just hide
I feel so sick deep down inside

I'm just getting thru the day
Won't someone hear a word I say?
I'm just getting thru the day
Hope that things will go my way

Excuses, excuses, my time is running out
My landlord evicts me it's time to move on out

I'm just getting thru the day
I'm just getting thru the day

HEARTBEAT OF A SPIDER

Like a faded chalk dust outline of someone who once existed
But for fate, he surely may have missed it

For someone who should be listed, you should not resist it

Like teardrops in the snow that had nowhere to go
Like a summer's breath that has nothing left

Like the heartbeat of the Spider
That nobody ever hears
Sitting in the corner for all those many years
Like the heartbeat of a spider
That no one knew existed
Was it really there at all?

Like sweat in the sand, I once had a band
They were hot but slipped from my hand

If I knew that you existed I thought you would be listed
But for you, my fate would have twisted

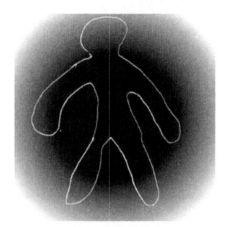

CENSORSHIP

Now you hear me, then you don't
First you see me and then you won't
My lines are sensual. My lines are straight
I'm the one the authorities hate

Cut, cut, snip, snip. My name is censorship
Censorship, censorship. My name is censorship
Cut, cut, snip, snip. My name is censorship
Censorship, censorship, censor, censorship

Ban me here. Ban me there
Do you think I really care?
Ban my records. Ban my tapes
You should be living with the apes

Cut, cut, snip, snip. My name is censorship
Censorship, censorship. My name is censorship
Cut, cut, snip, snip. My name is censorship
Censorship, censorship, censor, censorship

Mary, Mary quite contrary
Does anyone really want to know?
Mary, Mary quite contrary.
Where will your public go?

Cut, cut, snip, snip. My name is censorship
Censorship, censorship. My name is censorship
Cut, cut, snip, snip. Say NO to censorship
Censorship, censorship, censor, censorship

OVER AND OVER

Look at me am I your desire?
I've got a line for you. Don't play with fire
Just listen out and I'll take you higher

Eyeliner and makeup, the look the shake up
Over and over, over and over
Over and over, over and over again

Good times and bad times, good tunes and bad rhymes
Friend to friend to the bitter end

You love me you hate me
You use me you make me
Over and over, over and over
Over and over, over and over again

Just when it looks like it's coming to an end
You push me to the edge and drive me around the bend
Then you come up, like a special friend

Over and over, over and over
Over and over, over and over over and over, over and over

LOVE ON THE PHONE

I believe in me, I believe in you boy
It ain't what we say, it's what we do boy
The public don't mind, all of the time
They need something to occupy their minds

I believe in me, I believe in you boy
It ain't what we say, it's what we do boy

Love on the phone
Passion thru the wires reaching your zone
Red-hot wires free the chill from your bones
Love on the phone, love on the phone

You got the look, you've got the thought boy
You know it's true, you want some more boy
Put your barriers down and I'll see you around
Let yourself go and never say no

Love on the phone
Passion thru the wires reaching your zone
Red-hot wires free the chill from your bones
Love on the phone, love on the phone

I feel like I've found a missing part
You've just discovered the key to my heart
I feel like we've just begun
The two of us could become like one

Love on the phone

MR. THUMBS DOWN

Welcome to mister thumbs down
We all know he is just a clown
Always wearing a permanent frown
Because he's mister thumbs down

Always looking to turn a positive into a negative
Because of you, fragile people need a sedative
Causing misery wherever you go
At least that's what you hope as you live in your own deluded show

Always running around town
Your mister thumbs down
But nobody really knows you
But you'll get your due

It's a sad existence to get your kicks from other's resistance
Because you are really non-existent
But when you are gone nobody will remember you
Not even a Facebook mention for all your bad intention. Boo hoo

Goodbye mister thumbs down
Don't you know that you're just a clown
Always wearing a permanent frown
Because your mister thumbs down

WE ARE THE FUTURE

In the year 2222
Life is boring, with nothing much to do
Take me back on a time machine
To a century that I've never seen
Please take me to an interesting year
Relief from the void that we call 'here'

We are the future, we are the future, we are the future

We walked amongst you for many a year
Afraid to be imprisoned by ignorance and fear
Early on some were burnt at the stake
Just to be honest could be a mistake

We are the future, we are the future, we are the future

What good is power if there's no-one to rule?
Think about it, yeah think about it
What good is money if there's nowhere to spend it?
Think about it, yeah think about it
What good is terror if there's no-one to terrify?
Think about it, yeah think about it
What good's a food mountain if there's no-one to eat it?
Think about it, yeah think about it
Think about it. Think about it!

You are. We are. You are. We are.
The future. The future.
You are the future. We are the future

PENICILLIN PASSION

Too many in one night
I just don't put up a fight
It taught me a lesson and gave me a fright

Penicillin passion
Penicillin passion
I liked a lot but now I'm on ration

Penicillin passion
Penicillin passion
Love for me is out of fashion
All because of penicillin passion

Walking in the waiting room
It's despondency and gloom
So this is love or lust in bloom

All because I'm hooked on penicillin passion

Now I'm without that Ivory tower
Oh how I miss that passion shower
Seeds of lust won't grow my flower

Penicillin passion. Penicillin passion
I liked a lot but now I'm on ration

If you got V.D the treatment is free
If you got V.D the treatment is free

SAD WORLD

Kokoa konashi sikai, kokoa konani konashi sikai

It's a sad world. It's such a sad world
It's not a dream world. It's such a mean world
Fruit machine high, pub scene low
Life slips by, it's go go go

You've got a sad face
You need a loving embrace
It's not such a great place
This thing they call the human race
Cigarette high, heroin low
Life slips by, it's the same old show

Does anyone learn from the things that they do?
Your life's a mistake but you think it's not you
Blame someone else for mistakes that you make
It's the easy way out, the only option to take

It's a sad world. It's such a sad world
Does anyone learn from the things that they do?
Does anyone learn from the things that they do?

El monde triste torotoro. Et el monde triste torotoro
Eisteine triegern velte . Eisteine triegern ertso velte
Einai luphmenov o kosmov. Poli luphmenov o kosmov
Laisser un triste monde. Laisser ti un triste monde
Kokoa konashi sikai. kokoa konani konashi sikai

THIS GUN'S FOR HIRE

Put your best wish under your pillow tonight
And hold on till the morning light
It's so good. It's so bad. It's so happy. It's so sad

This gun's for hire. Give me love or I'll fire
You out of my life, out of my dreams, forever

Bark at the Moon tonight
Why don't you give your neighbours a fright?
Let me see your razorblade smile
Leaking laughter for a while

This gun's for hire. Give me love or I'll fire
You out of my life, out of my dreams, forever

Be my private eye and I will always try
And I'll never lie and never say goodbye

This gun's for hire. Give me love or I'll fire
You out of my life, out of my dreams, forever

ELECTRICITY ECCENTRICITY

Under the covers at night, I always put up a fight
With only a torch as my guiding light
My imagination was burning bright
It took a lot to focus my sight

Yes it was the torch that showed me the way
to write my special essay

No electricity on eccentricity
It's not a mystery, I made my own history.
Eccentricity has its own electricity
Burning a path through my own history
Electricity, eccentricity, electricity

I could never be a writer I was told
As I shivered in the cold
A pen stuck to a glove looking to be so bold
I was born to write even though I was not so old

I was a writer under the cover of night
It's when my imagination always took flight
With only a torch as a guiding light
I got it wrong but in the end, I got it so right

Every time I hear a yell
I always think eggshell
I was cracking up, not so well
Please someone rescue me from this hell.

No electricity on eccentricity
It's not a mystery, I made my own history
Eccentricity has its own electricity
Burning a path through my own history
Electricity, eccentricity, electricity

MOD CHRISTMAS

Sitting by the fire because it's cold outside

Think it's time to take my scooter for a ride

It's a way of life I take in my stride

No matter what the resistance you'll never hold back the tide

It's going to be a Mod Christmas, It's going to be a Mod Christmas

It's going to be a Mod Christmas tonight

Tonight, tonight

Spending all my money on looking sharp

Dust off those old records, I'm gonna to dance all night

So get ready and hold me so tight

Because I want to hear my heart taking flight.

It's going to be a Mod Christmas . It's going to be a Mod Christmas

It's going to be a Mod Christmas tonight

Tonight, tonight

Oh, oh oh, oh, it's Christmas time, Oh, oh oh, oh, it's Christmas time

It's going to be a Mod Christmas

It's going to be a Mod Christmas

It's going to be a Mod Christmas tonight

Tonight, tonight

LOVE O'CLOCK

I'm just sitting here waiting on time
One O'clock, two O'clock, waiting on a sign
Counting down the minutes until you'll be mine
Every second counts in large amounts

I feel you are just a kiss away
Send me your passion, make my day

Bang bang, she knocked me off my feet
With a passionate kiss that was not discreet
Bang bang, I can feel the heat
From duelling hearts that never missed a beat

Hold the front page
I'm out of my cage
My emotions are on the rampage
I've been hired for a loving wage

Just waiting on time
One O'clock, two O'clock , yes one clock at a time
Dreaming minute upon minute until you'll be mine
It's the seconds that bond us in rhyme

Here I am just killing time
But it's time that's killing me
One kiss from you
Will set me free

BROKEN PEOPLE

My manager is drunk up in his bunk and talking a load of Junk
All I want to do is spill some spunk
My feet were itching
The world around me was becoming bewitching

I collect broken people
Smashed minds of different kinds
Damsels in distress, so many damsels in distress
Oh, their life is such a mess
But it doesn't make me love them less

So many people broken
Words can only be a token
So many people broken
No more words can be spoken

Another broken dream
You know what I mean
Another shattered life
I attract them and soak up their strife

Like bees to honey
I make their life more sunny
Like damaged goods lost in the wood
I seem to be their Robin Hood

I collect broken people
Broken people are me
I collect broken people
I am your family tree
I collect broken people
They all flock to me

THE LONG DROP

Crying in my sleep tonight
My loverboy has taken flight
He killed a man over me
Over jealousy, over jealousy
Yeah, jealousy

Well, it's the long drop for him today
Society says he has to pay
It's the long drop for our love as well
We all experience a different hell
Our own private hell

Now he's gone from my life
And I'll never be his wife
I look down at a knife
But something stops me deep inside
Something inside of me,
It's a second chance

Well it's the long drop for him today
Society says he has to pay
It's the long drop for our love as well
We all experience a different hell
It's the long drop
Our own private hell
Our own private hell

With contributions from Tony Kaye

MODS FOREVER

When you hear the opening riff to the M.G song
You know everybody's gonna sing along
All they want is to have some fun
Have some fffff Fun

Mods forever
Never say never
Always together
We're Mods forever

When you see the cut of a very sharp suit
You know straight away you've found your roots

Let's rally around
And get lost and found
Cool scooters make a heavenly sound
Custom mirrors shining all around

When you know how to dress
It relieves all stress
You're not like the others
Who look a mess

Because you're a Mod forever
Never say never
Always together
We're Mods forever

WELCOME TO MY LAND

Come inside, take a ride, feel the vibe
Of the mysteries of a different tribe
You can play, DNA, today
To switch on is the only way

Don't hide, open wide, be on my side
It's a feeling you don't want to hide
To be real is to feel the real deal
Now you know the big appeal

From the sea to a tree, could it be me?
Look around am I what you see?
Are you sad, am I mad, it's not so bad
It's the best situation that you've ever had

Welcome to my land
Across the river from the Rio Grand
From Roswell to Cancun
We will be amongst you soon

ATTITUDE

Kids today, just got no attitude
They think the big A is about being crude
But instead of being rude
Cast off your shackles and set the mood

You can't buy attitude from the pages of a magazine
It's not about dressing to be seen
It's not about tantrums or to shout and scream
People with real attitude can realise their dream

Rebel without a cause
Contracts without a clause
Time to stop and pause
Then be a rebel with a cause

MIXING WITH THE UNKNOWN

Mixing with the unknown
Shake hands with the dead zone
Now you're feeling all alone
Mixing with the unknown

I don't want to be mixing with the unknown
Not after the images I've been shown
My mind has been well and truly blown
All because I mixed with the unknown

A punk cell offers an eerie tone
I can't reach anyone on my phone
Walking through the dead zone
Mixing with the unknown

Mixing with the unknown
Feeling a chill along each & every bone
Everyone looks like a Freddy clone
The king of horror sits on his throne

None one can hear you moan
When you're mixing with the unknown
Drowned out by the zombie drone
That's mixing with the unknown

ALIENANTION BREAKDOWN

Alien, alienation breakdown
Life's circles going around and around
A common language can't be found
It sees me heading for cover underground
Heading for an Alien, alienation breakdown

Human emotions are making me drown
Never destined to wear a crown
It's not funny and I'm not your clown
Just want to hide under an invisible gown
I'm heading for an Alien, Alien breakdown

An artistic sanctuary I can't find
I'm under attack from a mediocre mind
Looking through me like they are blind
I'm trudging through a daily grind
In search of my peace of mind, peace of mind, peace of mind
No I can't find that piece of my mind that I left behind

The changeling is blending in
Like a splash of tonic in some gin
Another direction and another road to begin
A torn agenda lies in an empty bin.

But that's not me, no that's not that's me
It's not the way I want to be
My mind just wants to be real and be forever free
From human thoughts and collective worldwide debris

Alienation, alienation, alienation, alien, stagnation equals alienation
Take me to the last stop on the station away from alienation
Let me see my brothers and sisters at the Angel station
Goodbye to alienation from this once happy Alien

D & J

It's snowing outside, I pull the covers over my head and hide.

Another day closer to summer, less 9-5

Hey, hold on a minute

I was mister one minute to 9

The rebel without a tie

Who was seen by an envious eye

It was the time of my life

A three-way split

I was overdosing on clit

The fan was static but never erratic

I was the head of the team

The most rebellious they'd ever seen

Time to play at D & J

I even get pay at D & J

Everything was going my way at D & J

But then along came judgement day at D & J

And I was sent away from D & J

But special memories never fade away

I'll always remember D & J

GENIUS JONES

I'm becoming more like Mr Jones
I can feel it in my bones
Crossing all artistic zones
Yes, it's me and Mr Jones

What makes a genius?
Is there one in all of us?

They say genius is just one step away from insanity
But to me, it's just a reality
Living in hope, living in the sun
It can be fraught or it can be fun

Genius Jones, I love your bones
Let me try your skin on, let me live in your zone
I want to be like genius Jones

I'm feeling like the last Geisha standing
My knowledge of the arts expanding
Because you taught me the perfect landing
We should all know our branding

MOVE YOUR FEET

You lived for strippers, didn't you Jack?
They nearly gave you a heart attack
You liked to live life on the edge
It left you up on a window ledge

Looking down upon that street
No, you couldn't stand the heat
The pavement looked good enough to eat
And you always liked your whisky neat

Move your feet to the beat
The heartbeat of life is everyone you meet
Life's the adventure that you learn to greet
The footsteps of history weren't built on retreat.
Move your feet, move your feet

You live your life from 9-5
Rushing around just to survive
There's more to life than just being alive
Learn how to swim and learn how to dive

Move your feet, move your feet
The heartbeat of life is everyone you meet
The footsteps of history weren't built on retreat
Live the adventure and learn to greet
Learn from everyone you meet

Move your feet, move your feet

PAINTED SMILE

A secret life, a humdrum life, just another wife

Looking around at all the painted smiles
All around for miles and miles
Let's start the day, let's begin
Let's see what the cat dragged in

Things are not quite what they seem
People living the same old dream

How are you doing? I'm doing fine
But underneath you've crossed the line
How are you doing? I'm doing great
But in reality, you're about to break

Paint that smile one last time
You're running out of war paint and you're still in your prime
What's going on? You haven't committed a crime
All you ever wanted was for your stars to align

Another false dawn, another massive yawn
Your psyche feels well worn
Sometimes you wish you'd never been born

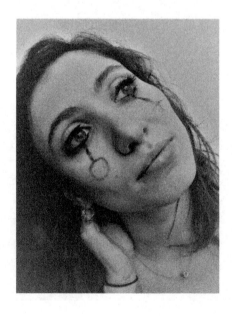

POETRY

Does it make you smile, does it make you cry?
Does it tell the truth, does it tell a lie?
That's Poetry

Does it wash over you like the sea on the beach?
Or does it inspire you to the furthest corners that you can reach?
That's Poetry

Did it change your life, did it cut like a knife?
Did it send you to sleep or did you follow the sheep?
That's Poetry

Did it make you think, did it make you blink?
Did you feel a link, did it take you away from the kitchen sink?
That's Poetry

If it does it for you, or did it do for me
Let's join together for a moment, let's all be free
That's Poetry

TRAILER PARK TRASH

Trailer park trash
Trailer park trash

You've been out on the lash
How many more times must you show your gash
They just want to put carpet burns all over your back
And introduce you to some addictive crack

Wake up you're not trailer park trash
Waiting for a bash followed by a hospital dash
Or looking for a handful of unwashed cash
Or a lowly job just slinging hash

Don't make the mistakes that your parents made
Strike out from under your self-made shade
You can do it and you don't need a blade
You can be a winner and get well paid

Trailer park trash
Trailer park trash

you'll be glad you made the dash
Or you'll have slowly turned to ash
Never again become trailer park trash

A TASTE OF HONEY (COMBS)

Time for Honey to keep the beat on Heaven street

To re-unite with Denis who was never a menace

They had the right to be in the top flight

Hit after hit, hitting height after height

That's the way the colour slides

Is it because talent never hides

These two may have passed away

But their music we shall always play.

This is a tribute to The Honeycomb's drummer Honey Langtree & lead vocalist Denis D'ell (to the right of Honey) whose last ever recorded release was produced by me in 1999 featuring the full original lineup, who reformed especially for me and played for the first time together in 20 years. They did a Bond cover of 'Live and Let Die'. It featured on the CD album 'Cult Themes from the 70's Vol.2' on Future Legend Records and on the download album 'The Theme's Bond ...James Bond (The Alternative Bond Themes)

The legendary Joe Meek produced their original big hits in the 60's including the worldwide No.1 'Have I the Right'. I am a huge fan of Joe as a producer as I too am an innovator like him. He was somewhat of a kindred spirit and someone I could relate to, although of course he was long gone before I arrived, having shot himself in 1967. So naturally, I was going to write a poem or song about him and it features on the next page.

SOMETIMES I FEEL LIKE JOE MEEK

I feel the pressure in my head
It must be the satellites overhead
Think I'll hide under my bed
My eyes are blurring and bloodshot red

There's a sound in my head
I don't know if it's living or dead
My production is out there... It's often said
When it comes to recording I go where others fear to tread

Sometimes I feel like Joe Meek
My mind explodes and I feel really weak
Sometimes I feel like Joe Meek
Lots of people think I'm a freak
Sometimes I feel like Joe Meek

The Telstar man had a masterplan
Footsteps on the stairs and voices in the can
Buddy Holly whispered in his ear
His vision was always crystal clear
He was never influenced by fear
He made records that lasted for more than one year

Don't look at me that way
Just get on and play
I'll make you a big star one day
But ignore me and it's 9-5 pay

Sometimes I feel like Joe Meek
My mind explodes and I feel really weak
Sometimes I feel like Joe Meek
Lots of people think I'm a freak
Sometimes I feel like Joe Meek

SENSORY ART

As apprehensions takes hold
May we be so bold
Our limits are untold
Emotions bought and sold

We suddenly connect with our intimate senses
Playing with past and present tenses
And project our reactions through this open door
Wanting more and more, we exude it from every pore

And now the dance can start
Welcome to Sensory Art
Tearing the rules apart
This is the world of Sensory Art
We always feel it in our heart
This is the world of Sensory Art

And we see colours come into life
Moving and curving like the dance of a pallet knife
Swapping from husband to wife
They surprise us with their eyes
It's a pleasant disguise

And now the dance can start
Welcome to Sensory Art
Tearing the rules apart
This is the world of Sensory Art
We always feel it in our heart
This is the world of Sensory Art

The perfume always lingers
When Maiko uses her fingers
Spreading the energy like a singer
Geisha R, arts dead ringer

And now the dance can start
Welcome to Sensory Art
Tearing the rules apart
This is the world of Sensory Art
We always feel it in our heart
This is the world of Sensory Art

Co written with Aurelie Freoua

NEW YEARS DAY

The sun shone thru an artistic window shutter
And we dared to utter
This will be our year
Have no fear

Then you began to say
Are you going my way
I wasn't but it seemed so right that day
It was like we were acting in a newly written play
Our thoughts were on display
It was a special soulmate kind of day
That new years day

We headed off to Notting Hill Gate
It was the first time you were never late
We have known for a while it was our fate
To often be as one whenever we create

Yes, the day started with shards of light through blinds
But it was soon soothing our minds
Just as well as my head was very tender
From this new years bender
But creative vibes never surrender
We always know how to render

KIDNAPPING TIME

Kidnapping Time, kidnapping time
I know you'll be mine, I know you'll be mine
Kidnapping Time, kidnapping timen
Let me draw our destiny line

I've travelled a thousand years
To heal your stinging tears
Till the end of time
I know you'll always be mine

Love, passion, affection
It was always our connection
Love, passion affection
It's coming in our direction
To kidnap you through time
And make the big correction

The poise of a Prince
The charisma of a Queen
It's always in the gene
I'm coming to get you
My life turns a nice shade of blue
But we are forever blond
Because we have a special bond

Love, passion, affection
It was always our connection
Love, passion affection
It's coming in our direction
To kidnap you through time
And make the big correction

THAILAND

It was the land of honey & sand
Her name was Bee and she held my hand
She started out being so tame
But by the end of the night, she felt no shame

A gangster's moll
Who once was a doll
The scar on her lip had taken its toll
Giving me pleasure was her final role

To her surprise, I made her cum
Her emotions suddenly came undone
For so many years she'd seen no sun
But I gave her a final bit of fun

She was a tailor
More used to getting the measure of a sailor
But she measured me and became a wailer

A torch song rang out in the night
Some lovers were having a fight
The flicker of love no longer burned bright
But a chalk dust outline was the final sight.

She was the girl with scrambled egg on her face
I wanted to lick it off and give her an embrace
She came from a faraway place
But always came with a vanity case
She had a secret life that left no trace
She found me very hard to replace

HE WROTE YOU KNOW

It's been a few years since he hit the limelight
Oh, since he enjoyed the high life
He wrote you know

He's got to stop the decline
Carve himself a new rythme
He wrote you know. He wrote you know. He wrote you know

Gotta get a new start again
Get some magic from that worn-out pen
That wrote you know

He goes to a plush affair
All the people stop and stare
Then someone says

He wrote you know

Is this not rotten
I've been gone but not forgotten
Because I wrote that song
Everybody knows the words and sings along

Yes, I wrote you know, I wrote you know

I wrote a new song today
I hope it gets some airplay
Then I can begin to say
I wrote a new song
And everyone sang along
And it wasn't you know. Yes it wasn't you know
It wasn't you know. It wasn't you know oh oh

WALLPAPER MAN

Tune into the wallpaper man, wallpaper man
He's about as exciting as watching paint dry
Tune into the wallpaper man, wallpaper man
He's got a personality like my carpet

The wallpaper man lacks a thought in his head
The wallpaper man's brain died a long long time ago
He thinks he's a brand
But the product he sells is ever so bland

Tune into the wallpaper man, wallpaper man
He's about as exciting as watching paint dry
Tune into the wallpaper man, wallpaper man
He's got a personality like my carpet

The wallpaper man's on daytime radio
The wallpaper man thinks he's a great show
The wallpaper man's got a thing in his hand
He likes to play with his gland

Tune into the wallpaper man, wallpaper man
He's about as exciting as watching paint dry
Tune into the wallpaper man, wallpaper man
He's got a personality like my carpet

The wallpaper man's on daytime radio
The wallpaper man thinks he's a great, great show
He thinks he's a brand
But his product is known to be bland

KNICKERS IN A BAG, FROG IN A BOX

Detox, detox, detox
Detox, detox, detox

I know a man, he's a twit, he's on Twitter
He used to be an ace bull-shitter

He had a piss, he had a shit
Now he's up to his thousandth hit

He did a rap, he was a rapper
Now his words belong down the crapper

Knickers in a bag, frog in a box
Let's all go to detox
Detox, detox,
Detox, detox

Knickers in a bag, frog in a box
Let's all go to detox
Detox, detox,
Detox, detox

He's going away for a twitter weekend
One thing's for sure, he will send and send

Knickers in a bag, frog in a box
Lets all go to detox
Detox, detox, detox detox

TEENAGE SEX

Some girls it makes them feel all right
Some girls it makes them up tight
She won't feel ashamed no more
She's not screwed up she wants some more

Some girls it makes them feel all right
Some girls it makes them up tight
Some girls think they just might
Teenage sex is flowing tonight
She won't feel ashamed no more
She's not screwed up she wants some more

Teenage sex is flowing tonight
Will she or won't she put up a fight
Agony aunts are going to get a fright
Teenage Sex is flowing tonight

Old fashion squares tell her
Don't do this and don't do that
Teenage sex is flowing tonight

She doesn't care what the people say
Hold her tight all night and day
She doesn't care what the people say
Life's full of heartache anyway

She doesn't care what the people say
Just hold her tight all night and day
Never care what the people say
It heals her heartache everyday

Never care what the people say. Teenage sex is flowing tonight

SKAG KIDS

Skag kids, oh skag kids

Skag kids, skag kids

Your lives on the skids

Open up your eyelids

When your life turns to shit

Will you take another hit?

Of the powder that makes you cry louder

Inside the postcard personality you've become

You're stuck in a groove you can't run

Skag kids, skag kids

Skag kids oh skag kids

You don't think twice

You're as meek as mice

But you're not so nice

no. you're not so nice

Skag kids, O skag kids

S O U L M A T E

Soulmate, Soulmate. Even my breath you understand

Soulmate, Soulmate, communication between our eyes is beyond truth
Through art we feel alive and fly so high and touch the sky
Arriving in a new reality of dreams, where we can be ourselves and make our
imagination grow

When we create, we catch ideas and visualize them coming to life
We could stay forever on our clouds of inspiration, surfing on a wave of thoughts

Ideas flow like a river and time becomes an illusion and everything timeless.
Memories are sources of inspiration. We balance between past, present and future
Time doesn't exist anymore and we are floating in space

You're reading my mind and feel the intensity of my emotions
We are travelling so deep into our souls that we are almost reaching the center of the
earth and directly connected to the energy of the universe
Our souls vibrate and resonate with each other

This is the journey of artistic soulmates, a journey where both minds become one and
are transformed into a creation

Always trying to discover new ways to express the infinite inside our truth

This is not a lonely path anymore and we can hold anothers hand

We drive on roads with unknown destinations and put ourselves in danger facing the
world

Together, we are escaping and entering new dimensions.

We let ourselves jump from the cliff, where the wind comes to hold us and helping us
to fly. We are ready to fly

By Aurelie Freoua

* To see why this poem is not by me please read the article that follows

THE CASE OF POETRY Y SONG LYRICS

As a extra little something. This is my quick controversial thought on poetry
There are often discussions asking are song lyrics poetry and vice versa.
My opinion is certainly many song lyrics are banal repetitive drivel at one end of the
spectrum but at the other end of the scale are the songwriters who are better than
most poets. To prove my point I need only say; John Lennon, Bob Dylan, Bryan Ferry,
Ray Davies, Paul Weller and there are many more. Hardcore fans live and breathe
the lyrics more than the music (I encountered this early on in my songwriting career
and it really hit home).The aforementioned songwriters' lines resonate with me far
more deeply than any poem. Here are a few favourites.

*'Can you tell a man by the way he speaks or spells or is it more important the story he
tells'* : 'Mike Hugg (Manfred Mann Chapter 3)

'I'd rather be a free man in my grave than to live life as a puppet or a slave' : Jimmy
Cliff

'She's dressed to kill and guess whose dying' : Bryan Ferry

'It's the kidney machines that pay for the rockets and guns' : Paul Weller

Most people would quote John Lennon's Imagine but if you know John Lennon's
history it doesn't get any better than, *'Mother you had me but I never had you, Father
you didn't want me but I wanted you'*

The above JL song sums up his whole childhood in two lines and the ones before that
not only conjure up a great image but succinctly encapsulate a stance and a feeling
that is very powerful whilst telling a bigger story in that one line.

So why do I think song lyrics are better than poetry? The best song lyrics are concise
and to the point and even without music hit home in a very direct way such as the
ones mentioned but there are many more I could cite. Poetry can move you and
engross you but many poems meander along and are often way too long. There is a
very good reason songs via music releases sell far more than poetry books.

I did one multi-art event where people proclaimed to love poetry and I ended up doing
an impromptu poetry reading following another poet. His poem was long and
meandering and I could see some audience members wilting halfway through this 8-
minute epic and some even vacated the room. He got what could best be described
as polite applause then I followed him with my much shorter piece 'Numbers' taken
from one of my songs, I got a standing ovation and sold any poetry/photography
books I had off the back of it. All the other poet got was advice not to give up his day
job. I am just stating the facts here of what happened. I'm not saying his poem was
bad and mine was better but it does seem to me the best poetry, like any art gets a
reaction & the ultimate reaction is another person being moved and wanting to own it.

So what is good and what is bad poetry? It's like any art. I go to many art exhibitions and have had many shows as a photographer. Like many people, if a piece of art moves me I buy it, if it doesn't I don't.That's the bottom line

But you could question, are sales the judge of good or bad work? Then I cast my mind back to curators trying to sell me art, pushing the angle that it's an award-winning artist. I still thought the work was uninspiring and boring but to my amazement, someone bought it. Maybe they genuinely liked it, so I asked them why they bought it and what it was they liked about it, they couldn't really tell me but quoted the salesperson saying the artist was an award winner. So a sheep mentality via sales the world over can often sell anything but the best work sells itself in my opinion. I rarely ever mention in person that I'm an award winner. I'd rather people buy what I do because it moves them or they love it. Although I know the odd person has bought something because they know I'm collectable and see it as an investment but that's kind of cool in its own way. But those sort of sales are the minority. Ironically it is usually others that make money off my work becoming collectible not necessarily me, although it increases my worth for new works.

Of course in the poetry world, like the publishing and art world, there can be a lot of snobbery about what poetry is good and what is not.

As I say about any art form, do it first because you like doing it or are compelled to do it and it makes you feel good. That is success right there and if it's good in your eyes it doesn't matter if anyone else likes it. Then if people like it that's a reward but the biggest reward in the times we live in is to have someone pay for your work making you a true professional, which leads to being established. Likes on the Internet don't pay the bills and people are too quick to press 'like' without even checking something out, so in my opinion, it has no value unless it translated into the person who clicked 'Like' becoming the owner of that work.

Until this year I would definitely have called myself a lyricist or songwriter more than a poet but with what has transpired this year I can say I'm a true poet as my work has moved people, sold and got standing ovations. So, I can now add poetry with pride to the list of arts I'm established in.

So, although I rate songwriters highly do I actually like any poets? Well, John Cooper Clark is the best ever but unknown emerging poets like Jade Evans are very good and I love her conviction and interesting subject matter, so keep an eye out for her but my favourite actual poem is by my Muse who is also my Maiko (Aurelie Freoua) who is an established artist often called the John Coltraine or Miles Davis of Abstract Art. I am biased of course as she says she wrote it about me but even if it wasn't about me I would still love it. She was keen to become a songwriter, so I edited her poem down to become a song and it features on the new Psykick Holiday album 'Sensory Art'. So included it as the last poem in my book. The full length version will be in her own poetry book (out next year) so keep an eye out for that release. Talking of the 'Sensory Art' album, I think I managed to do the perfect hybrid of traditional poetry meets song lyric meets book intro into an 8-minute song and it has made a big impact' It is called 'Life's Great Adventure' which kicked off this book.

Russell is an established Multi-Platform Artist from London who has made a dent in all the arts, often setting new trends like the Cult Themes craze as well as pioneering new music genres but writing has always been his first love. Before turning 16 he got a job as a DJ at night and continued with that nocturnal career whilst during the day learning the ropes at ATV Television under the guidance of legendary TV impresario Lord Lew Grade, after impressing him with some early scripts he'd written. Through this contact, he sold his first film script at 17 (Starstruck) in no lesser place than Hollywood. He then managed 'Music Master' record shop in London, making it extremely successful. Around this time, an international agency noticed him and signed him up and he began to DJ all around Europe eventually becoming the No.1 D.J in Scandinavia. He then met and married British pop singer 'Eleanor Rigby' and changed his career to become a songwriter/record producer for her. He has since had 400 releases worldwide with various artists as a music producer including a number-one European hit 'You Only Live Twice'. Many records he has produced are also very collectable and he is often called the new Joe Meek because of his innovative approach to recording and top UK national newspaper The Independent called him 'An Indie production God'. He has also been previously been nominated for UK record producer of the year. (he sometimes produces under the alias Russell Writer). He has had over 70 song releases and was recently on the front cover of Songwriter International magazine He has also won an international poem of the year award. He invented the pop noir genre of music (jazz/punk attitude, classical ambience, hypnotic grooves, poignant lyrics and filmic feel) and his band Psykick Holiday who released the innovative 'Forever Pop Noir' album and a series of singles with Russell playing the unique Punk Cello & doing some vocals. A recent solo concert got one of the best reactions he has ever had and he is looking forward to doing more, preferably with Psykick Holiday to promote their new album' Sensory Art' due out in early 2023.

He also wrote and edited the cult publication 'Dedicated Follower'. Original copies are now housed in the prestigious Victoria and Albert Museum in London after it featured in a cultural exhibition there. After a long gap, it was recently re-launched for the lockdown period and has proved extremely popular with 13 issues released in physical form so far.

He also penned the infamous book 'Music Business Bastards (How to do well in the Music Business without getting ripped off)' published in the 90's, by Martin Breese Publishing which helped many artists along the way. It has been updated and released twice more with equal success by December Books UK. 14 further books followed both fiction and non-fiction.

He also ran a successful Indie record label 'Future Legend Records ' The legendary Tony Wilson (Factory Records) called his label the definitive Indie label. (Next year is its 30th anniversary) He was also in a few influential pioneering pop groups influencing many famous bands that followed. (Particularly in the Britpop era)

Russell initially stumbled into photography; doing some highly rated record sleeves, posters and several iconic photos of Eleanor, some calling him the new David Bailey. He has had several exhibitions. Saatchi Art called him an artist of recognition. Two limited-edition books 'Voyeurs Welcome' Vol.1 & 2 were released featuring his photography and lyrics/poetry and sold out in a few weeks and are very collectable fetching high prices. Four novels have also been released. Some have gotten Hollywood interest. Using his musical knowledge and expertise, he wrote the popular 'Memories Are Made of This' (The Ultimate Retro Quiz) 50s to 90s, that hit the Amazon top 100. Three more in the series have been released, with the latest one being an in-depth one on films. On the non-fiction side, a limited edition 'The Definitive Eleanor Rigby Story' biog sold out in less than a week. Another biog; The Box Office Poison Story has just been released. He has also directed and edited over 100 pop videos, plus a TV show and documentary. He is moving more into films in the future as a writer/director to complete the whole artistic circle of accomplishments but cites writing as his first love.

Also amongst his fans are Madonna, Brian Wilson, David Bowie, Shirley Manson & John Barry, with the latter saying Russell even produced some Bond tracks better than him.

There is much more but this is a flavour. More at the website address in book credits.

MEMORIES ARE MADE OF THIS

The below 4 books in the 'Memories Are Made of This' series by Russell. Two are retro pop trivia quizzes 50s to 90s with lots of extra trivia to impress your friends with. As you'd expect with Russell being a former DJ, Record shop manager and head of a record label his knowledge is pretty extensive (He used to regularly clear out pub trivia machines that had pop questions). Many other pop quizzes are very predicatble and often bland but this one has humour plus thousands of easy, medium & hard questions. The next one was more nitche as Russell grew up a Mod and knows that scene & its music very well, so that one is a must for any Mod or Britpoppers.
The final book centered around film and is perhaps the best of all 4 books with not just quiz questions but loads more trvia, critiques of key films & concetraing on 100 years of film including best of lists with additional write ups on each and great photos & posters.

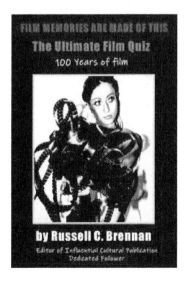

MUSIC BUSINESS BASTARDS (How to do well in the Music Business without getting ripped off). Updated version.

Russell is somewhat of a music expert, having worked on most sides of the music industry. He hates to see people get ripped off or used so penned this informative book that helped a number of bands and solo artists kick off their careers and save them heartache and money. It has been successfully released on 3 occasions and this is the most up to date version for the internet generation. It also gives positive and insightful advice about standing out from the competition. It is a must read for anyone serious about making it in the music business. It ends by delivering a chilling tale about the demise of the music industry and gives both a positive and negative ways forward for the industry and new people entering into it.

OVER AND OVER (Novel)

Over and Over is a modern day noir style story of singer-songwriter Nikki North.

Far from it being the bog standard Cinderella story of rags to riches after a great singer is discovered by some Prince Charming or a comedy, this story tells it the way it really is in the music industry.

It takes you on a journey through the seedy shark-infested backwaters of the music industry with a shady character frequenting every other doorway, waiting to take advantage of the next hopeful floating by. It's feeding time and Nikki is on the menu.

After being used and abused by the music industry, enough is enough, something has to snap and it's Nikki. Anyone getting in her way will find themselves in Shit Street with not a glimpse of toilet paper in sight. Revenge is on the agenda and low lives that initially used her will wish they had never been born. The story is rich with sharply drawn characters and realistic dialogue with incidents around every corner.

This book is about to be made into a major feature film but this novel features extra bits not in the film and a slightly different slant to it

ADVENTURES OF A DARK DUKE: THE PIN (Novel)

This is a contemporary story of a British indie pop star who lives a secret life as an adventurer. Looking for material for new songs and hooked on adventure, Duke sticks a pin in a map and follows it religiously for a month to have the adventure of a life time, with Florida, Cuba and Mexico making up the colourful backdrop.

From danger with a stranger to a poignant love story, to a hidden Hollywood A-list sect, the stories and characters keep on coming and so does he, for he likes to live a very erotic lifestyle and living life on the edge is what it's all about otherwise he is taking up too much room.

The book is like a Russian doll with stories within stories that have many twists and turns. It's full of colourful characters who often have a unique way with words.

It is often told in the first person narrative making it like virtual reality for books.

So, if the title name conjures up a 'Mills and Boon' romantic royal character, sorry to disappoint – thats is not what's on offer here. This is a novel for those who don't shy away from erotic content and like something a bit original, more cutting edge and very contemporary.

Rumour has it that it may also be based on a true story and this is the first in the 'Adventures of a Dark Duke' series of fiction.

This book has 100% all 5 star reviews at Amazon UK. Here are a few headlines.

"Simply Brilliant! It will be hard to find a better read this year" (O)
"Addictive reading! It keeps you on your toes." (MD)
"**Fantastic Novel**! Original, exciting, hypnotic & erotic. A must read." (SC)
"**A book you want to read**! Entertaining & exciting. A real page turner." (SG)
"Great read! It's not often a book exceeds expectations, this one certainly did."(A)
The best book I've read in a very, very long time" (KG

KIDNAPPING TIME (novel)

Kidnapping Time is an exciting erotic Sci-Fi conspiracy thriller.

Descendants of H.G. Wells & Leonardo Da Vinci build a Time Machine based on their famous ancestors' works. Rather than go through history eliminating evil dictators they decide they'd rather make love to the sexiest women in history instead.

However, they get more than they bargained for as they get caught up in some of the most famous conspiracies of the last 3,000 years from Cleopatra to Elizabeth 1st and beyond, with Marilyn Monroe, Bridget Bardot, Jane Fonda, Princess Diana, The Kennedy's and many more household names front and centre of some very interesting storylines. It also features a very poignant love story between Marilyn & Frank Sinatra as a core story.

The novel features lots of thrills and twists plus the author's trade mark tasteful ultra-erotic element. Although not a comedy story it has more funny moments in just one chapter than most comedy feature films, such as when Marilyn is kidnapped through time to this Century and even struggles to get a job as an M.M look-alike! The book is full of water-cooler moments that will leave you on a high with a smile on your face. If you are already a fan of any of the characters mentioned, you'll love this book but always remember this is Science Fiction and although some things may seem familiar they are not always as they seem. History will never be the same again!

THE BOX OFFICE POISON STORY (Biography)

What do David Bowie, Madonna, John Barry and Brian Wilson know that you don't? They must know something, as they were all fans of Box Office Poison. Dig just beyond the surface of the music business and you will find the true pioneers of music genres and music trends. Box Office Poison or to be more precise their main man Russell C. Brennan, invented the Pop Noir genre of music that influenced the likes of Goldfrapp and others. He also started the Cult Themes trend in the 90s and Ska Surf music. He was even one of the catalysts for Britpop via the classic album 'Censorship' that he wrote and produced for cult artist Eleanor Rigby that many Britpop bands have cited as an influence. Unlike other bands biogs that are pretty much a merry go round of recording, tours, drugs and rows, Box Office Poison had a far more interesting story during their 10-year existence, with extreme ups and downs. Also, amongst the definitive line up lurked the brilliant sexy vocalist Misty Woods who could give any of today's female singers a lesson in real star quality. If you like a name drop there was also sax player Ron Howe in the ranks, formerly of The Cure, Fools Dance (and occasionally The Damned). This biography is a warts and all tale featuring guest appearances from many interesting characters in the music business, including some very famous names, including, David Bowie, Madonna, John Barry, Brian Wilson, Don Arden, Mickie Most and more. Also, a somewhat unconventional love triangle as well. As a bonus, Russell also incorporates behind the scenes in-depth info about his innovative production on many cult themes tracks he produced for various bands (via 7 albums) including some number one hit acts. This culminated in him being lauded as the new Joe Meek and being nominated for UK Record Producer of the year and UK national newspaper calling him an indie production god. If you love music biogs, cutting edge music, drama, history or trivia this is a good book to spend some time with. It is also a good lesson to learn from, for upcoming acts. Oh and naturally it contains many rare photos including the two sexy indie pop pin-ups in the band, Misty Woods & Mouse..

THE DEFINITIVE ELEANOR RIGBY STORY (biog)

'Bursting onto the world of music with a very controversial debut single to releasing a classic album that influenced all the big names in Britpop to disappearing at the height of her popularity, this is one of the most controversial stories in pop music. '.

The book contains 50% new exclusive behind the scenes info about cult artist Eleanor and many elaborations on the basic controversial story many may know. Plus rare and unseen exclusive photos and for early birds the last unreleased music track by the girl herself never heard by anybody except her other half Russell, who is the only one in a position to tell this unique story that has everything you would want from a warts and all biography. Intrigue, mystery, controversy, a love story, big success but also massive setbacks. A unique peek into the back-room of how the music business works.

As with anything Eleanor Rigby this book will be limited edition and be deleted fairly quickly after release. It will not be available via any bookshop or on Amazon and will only be on paperback not kindle, you can only get it via by emailing her record label address below. Only 1,000 paperbacks will be available. All will be signed by the author. The first 500 people get an MP3 of Eleanor's unheard and unreleased music track. .Eleanor has 10 times the amount of followers as there are books available so it will pay to get in quickly with this release and avoid paying collectors price a year from now.

futurelegend2000@yahoo.co.uk

MIXING WITH THE UNKNOWN (Novel)

Original horror books are hard to come by but 'Mixing with The Unknown' might just break the mould. In a nutshell, it's traditional horror meets 'Pulp Fiction' with some new twists on horror staples plus lashings of erotica.

John Spencer is a seasoned film scriptwriter of horror. He is jaded and looking for a new challenge and is offered a book publishing deal if he can come up with a different slant on the horror genre. He sets about writing 'Mixing With The Unknown' but stretching his mind to it's limit tips him over the edge leading to dire consequences for characters he encounters as well as himself.

The extra twist is anyone buying the book gets to experience first-hand the chapter of the book they like best and a nightmare scenario begins for many readers who are all loosely entwined with each other like the film 'Pulp Fiction'.

As well as new Urban Horror the book features new twists on Vampires, Possession, Ouija Boards, Ghosts, Witchcraft & Voodoo.

This novel also brings another extra to the table in the way of ultra erotica, which is one of author Russell C. Brennan's trademarks (if you have read other novels by him you will know what to expect).
The erotic element that was in traditional horror seems to have been lost over the years if todays horror films are anything to go by. The emphasis seems to be on violence and gore more and directors and writers often shy away from nudity never mind sex. When Dracula first appeared there was an erotic element to it in both books and films and many a teenage boy would queue up for some naked flesh and brief sex scene (Which of course look tame today) via Hammer Horror films from the last century.
The bottom line for any worthwhile book is it is very much story driven affair.

DEDICATED FOLLOWER

Russell is the editor and main writer of the influential zine Dedicated Follower. It did well when originally released as it was featured in a V & A Museum exhibition on UK culture & that's where original copies now reside. After shelving it for a long time he brought it back just before the lockdown and it became very popular in paper form during the pandemic (people were getting fed up with being online & phones) Several issues came out featuring many interesting articles & interviews For more info about each issue visit the website
https://dedicated-follower.co.uk

FUTURE LEGEND RECORDS

Many of the poems/lyrics you have read in this book feature in song releases. Artists covering them including Eleanor Rigby, Misty Woods, Box Office Poison, Psykick Holiday, Glenda Collins & others who can be found on Future Legend Records website. (A few album sleeves are below) FLR are also known for excellent covers of Cult Themes music. If you have taken a shines to any images in the book and want to see more, these feature at https://dedicated-follower.co.uk/artistandalien.htm
Alternatively, visit Russell's personal website to see his top images (link at front of the book)

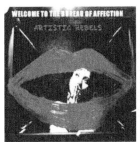  

Printed in Great Britain
by Amazon

19750752R00061